Take up
Canoeing

Take up Sport

Titles in this series currently available or shortly to be published:

Take up Canoeing

Principal contributor:
Ray Rowe
British Canoe Union Coach
and former Head of Canoeing
at the National Centre for Mountain Activities,
North Wales

SPRINGFIELD BOOKS LIMITED

Copyright © Springfield Books Limited and White Line Press
1990

ISBN 0 947655 83 2

First published 1990 by
Springfield Books Limited
Springfield House, Norman Road, Denby Dale, Huddersfield
HD8 8TH

Edited, designed and produced by
White Line Press
60 Bradford Road, Stanningley, Leeds LS28 6EF

Editors: Noel Whittall and Philip Gardner
Design: Krystyna Hewitt
Diagrams: Steve Beaumont

Printed and bound in Great Britain

Photographic credits
Cover photograph: Action Plus
British Canoe Union (BCU): 14, 39 (br), 43
British Sports Association for the Disabled: 33
John Draddy: 27
Evening Standard/BCU: 41 (t)
B. Greenaway: 39 (2t)
Mrs D. Horrocks: 44, 45
Paul Keable/BCU: 21, 42
Keith Price/Ray Rowe: 9, 16, 17, 20, 46 (t), 54, 57
Richard Robinson: 60
Ray Rowe: 13, 15, 19, 23, 39 (bl), 46 (b), 47, 49, 56, 58
Tee Pee Photography/BCU: 41 (b)
Noel Whittall: 6, 52, 59

Contents

Introduction

Canoeing is a very special kind of sport. It offers a whole range of activities, from Olympic competition to touring in wild and beautiful country. Anyone can take up canoeing: girls and boys, men and women; there are four-year-olds and there are eighty-four-year-olds involved in the sport.

A canoe is a fascinating craft: it's easy to transport to any piece of water you like, and simple to propel once on the water. It is also one of the cheapest forms of boat available. Travelling by canoe is good healthy exercise which lets you enjoy the natural world without causing harm or pollution.

People with visual and physical handicaps can also enjoy canoeing. Several craft are now available which have been designed specifically for this purpose, and able-bodied and disabled paddlers can easily share the sport by using double craft.

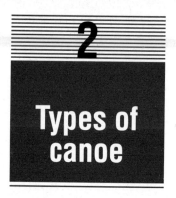

2

Types of canoe

There are many different types of canoe available today. The range might look overwhelming at first, but the reasons for each design shape and construction are quite simple. Whatever their differences, all canoes are *paddled* along, and — unlike oarsmen — paddlers enjoy the benefit of facing in the direction in which they are travelling.

Canoes and kayaks

There are two main groups of craft which make up the canoe family: *canoes* and *kayaks*. Confusingly, paddling in either form of craft is commonly known as *canoeing*, but the following explanations should help you to sort them out.

A *canoe* is a boat in which the paddler may either kneel or sit. Canoes are propelled by a paddle with a single blade. They were originated by the Native Americans, who used skin or birch bark to form the outer shell.

In a *kayak*, the paddler sits in a cockpit enclosed by a deck, and propels the boat with a double-bladed paddle. Kayaks were first used by the Eskimos (Inuit), who found that the rapid acceleration and silent movement of the boat was perfect when hunting walrus and seal. The shells of the original kayaks were made from greased skins.

All the boats in this book fit into one or other of these categories, and you will very soon be able to spot which is which without having to think about it.

Canoes and kayaks fall into two further categories: those used for competition and those designed for other purposes.

Most canoeing is done in single-seaters, but there are double and even four-person boats available. Variety is very much a part of canoeing, and it is the diversity of the craft and of the experiences possible in them that makes it popular with so many people.

A flat-water racing single kayak. Note the very slim lines and small rudder at the rear.

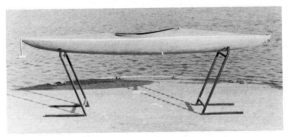

A non-competition white-water kayak. This is a rugged design capable of giving years of good service in tough conditions.

An open canoe, frequently called a Canadian canoe. This design offers plenty of space, and may be paddled either single or double.

A single-seat sea-touring kayak. The three round black rubber covers give access to the sealed storage compartments beneath the deck.

Design features

All canoes are relatively slim when viewed from above, but some are much slimmer than others. You can tell the purpose of a particular craft by looking at a few basic features:

- If the boat is long and thin, it will run straight and fast on the water and will be rather difficult to turn. Canoes and kayaks designed for still-water sprinting come into this category. Newcomers find them rather "tippy" to paddle at first, but you soon get used to this, and the slick effortless way the boat slips through the water has a compulsive appeal. Most racing kayaks are steered by a rudder at the rear which is controlled by the paddler's feet on a tiller bar.

- When speed of turning is more important than all-out speed, a boat which is relatively short and wide will give the best response. As slalom racers require a boat which will spin and manoeuvre easily around poles or rocks, the hulls of their boats tend to be quite flat in cross-section. No rudders are fitted to this type of canoe or kayak — all the steering is done with the paddles — and the beginner's first impression is usually that it is very difficult to follow a straight course! This is frustrating for the first half hour or so, but with a little practice you quickly learn how to keep control.

- Carrying capacity may be important for non-competitive canoes and kayaks. The open canoe (sometimes called the Canadian canoe) is outstanding in this respect: its virtually deckless form allows huge quantities of equipment to be stowed. It makes an excellent travelling vessel in which long journeys in wilderness country are possible. The space can also be used for passengers, making the Canadian canoe a safe and sociable way of introducing whole families or groups to the sport.

Many forms of craft combine several of these design features to suit the job in hand. The sea-touring kayak is a good example. It is long and thin, for speed, but has a cross-section which is deep enough to allow equipment to be stored. The space that forms the storage compartments can be sealed; this aids the kayak's buoyancy, helping it to rise out of the waves in rough seas.

Internal flotation

It is absolutely essential that any canoe or kayak you use is capable of staying afloat when flooded with water. This is normally achieved by securing flotation material (usually buoyant foam) or air bags into the inside of the boat at either end. All reputable manufacturers ensure that this basic safety feature is incorporated into their boats. When purchasing second-hand craft, always check for yourself that the internal flotation is still intact, even if the boat appears to be in perfect condition.

If you are in any doubt about flotation, buoyant foam or air bags may be bought and secured into a boat at any stage.

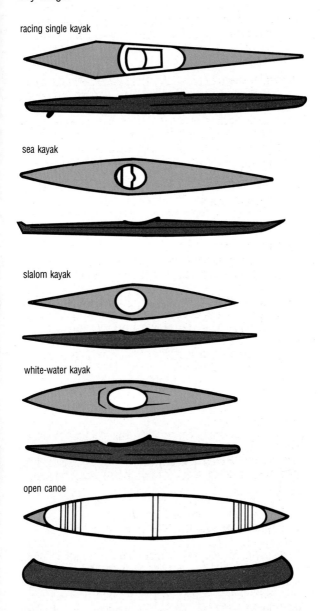

racing single kayak

sea kayak

slalom kayak

white-water kayak

open canoe

Figure 1 Some different designs of canoes and kayaks

Figure 2 A typical kayak suitable for a range of activities, including white-water kayaking

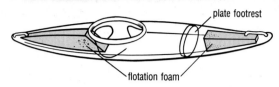

plate footrest

flotation foam

Footrest

All kayaks need to have a footrest of some kind: you simply cannot paddle properly without one, since much of the thrust used in propelling the boat comes from the resistance of the footrest. Footrests come in various forms, and they are usually adjustable, so that paddlers of different leg lengths can use the kayak. White-water paddlers require a specially strong footrest in the form of a plate: this is to prevent them from slipping forward if their kayak hits an obstacle in front.

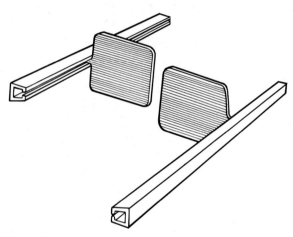

Figure 3 A popular type of adjustable footrest system: the tracks bolt into the boat on either side, and the pedals adjust independently

Construction materials

Fibre-reinforced plastics

Modern canoes and kayaks are usually constructed from plastics of various forms. Glass-reinforced plastic (GRP), sometimes called *fibreglass*, remains very popular, although more modern reinforcing fibres such as Kevlar and carbon are increasingly used. These "high-tech" materials are commonest in lightweight flat-water and slalom racing.

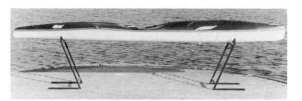

A lightweight wild-water racer constructed from GRP.

Boats using reinforced plastics are built by laying a mat of resin-impregnated fibre against a mould, and allowing it to cure. It is still possible to hire a mould and build your own boat using this process, and this can be an inexpensive way for a beginner to get afloat.

Polyethylene

A vast number of non-competitive white-water kayaks are now produced in polyethylene. This is softer than GRP, but more durable overall. Polyethylene boats have to be commercially produced, but they are excellent value for money and ideal for beginners.

This paddler seems determined to test his polyethylene kayak to the limit!

Wood

Many years ago, most canoes were made from wood. However, the expense of the material, the high standard of craftsmanship needed during construction, and the need for careful maintenance, have led to the rise in popularity of plastics. However, some top racing kayaks and a range of open canoes are still manufactured in timber.

3

Equipment and clothing

As with every other sport, canoeing equipment is produced in various qualities, and this means a choice of prices. It is not necessary for a beginner to use top-quality equipment, and you should save your money until you have decided what aspect of the sport you wish to specialise in. The exception to this is your personal buoyancy aid (see page 17). I strongly recommend that you buy a good one of these at the outset.

Kayak paddles

Almost all kayak paddles have their blades offset at about ninety degrees. The reason for this is simply to let the blade which is not in the water slice through the air easily.

This photograph clearly shows how the blades of a kayak paddle are offset relative to each other. This is referred to as being feathered.

Racing paddles are made from carbon fibre and other expensive materials which give a combination of strength and lightness. A more suitable paddle for beginners has an alloy shaft with moulded plastic blades. This type is very durable and yet not excessively heavy.

A good paddle for a beginner. The blade is made from moulded plastic, and fitted to an alloy shaft.

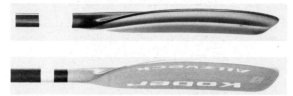

A composite blade for white-water use. These are more expensive than the moulded plastic blades.

Choosing your kayak paddle

It is important to choose a paddle which is of a length to suit your height. There is a simple way to check this:

Hold the paddle so that the mid-point of the shaft sits on top of your head. Move your hands equally from the mid-point until a right angle is formed at each elbow. This is the correct paddling grip for you. The distance from the outside of your hand to the start of the blade should be approximately 210 mm (8.25 in).

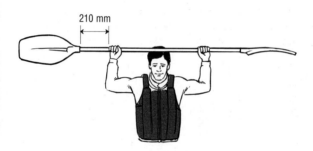

Figure 4 Choosing a kayak paddle of the right length.

Once you have your own paddle, mark the outer limits of your hand grip with tape. This ensures that you can feel when your hands are evenly and correctly placed while paddling.

The blades of kayak paddles are usually curved to improve their grip in the water. Flat blades are available, but I recommend that you go for the curved form. These come in right-handed and left-handed versions, and you will have to decide which suits you best. The general rule is that right-handed people prefer right-handed paddles, and vice versa. If you are in doubt, just hold the paddles in your normal grip and go through the paddling action (see page 24): you will find out at once what feels natural for *you*.

15

Canoe paddles

Canoe paddles come in a very wide range of shapes and sizes, many of them being hand-built in wood. Once again, a beginner can manage with a cheaper paddle which is made from the same alloy/plastic combination as the kayak paddle described earlier.

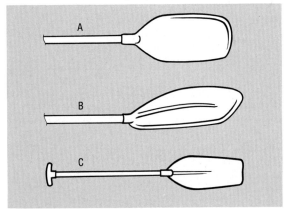

Figure 5 Paddle blades: *A* is a general-purpose kayak paddle; *B* is a kayak racing paddle also used in sea and inland touring; *C* is a canoe paddle.

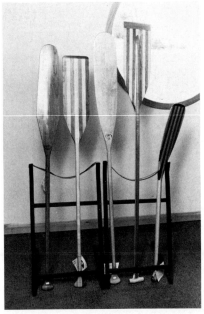

A selection of canoe paddles made from wood.

Check your canoe paddle for size by standing up-right holding the paddle in front of you with the tip of the blade touching the ground. The handle which forms the T-shaped grip should be level with your nose. All canoe paddles may be used by either right- or left-handed paddlers.

The above suggestions for choosing a paddle are general-purpose guidelines for beginners. Once you really start to specialise, your needs may change slightly because canoeing and kayaking disciplines have specific requirements concerning the length and shape of the paddles. Slalom kayak paddles, for example, are generally shorter than those used by flat-water racers.

Buoyancy aid

Make it a rule to wear a personal buoyancy aid every time you go canoeing, no matter how good a swimmer you are. Modern canoeing buoyancy aids contain soft flotation foam which moulds itself to your body. These are extremely comfortable, as they hardly restrict your movement at all, and in cold weather they provide superb insulation!

A buoyancy aid is an essential part of canoeing equipment.

Two things are important to check when buying a buoyancy aid:

● that the jacket fits snugly over your normal canoeing clothing

● that it has the mark of approval of a respected national or international agency. In Britain, look for one of the following marks:

    BCU/BCMA BA 83
    SBBNF/79
    BMIF Standard

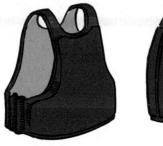

Figure 6 Two types of canoeing buoyancy aid

The buoyancy aid needs to be the right size and properly fitted. If it is too tight it will limit your movement; if it is too large, or if the waist draw-cord or belt has not been adjusted, it will slip upwards over your head if you fall into the water. Always secure it firmly before getting into your boat. A buoyancy aid which is not worn properly can easily become worse than none at all when you are in the water.

Do not be tempted to buy a secondhand buoyancy aid unless you are certain it is less than three years old. The foam which provides the buoyancy deteriorates with age and general wear-and-tear. As your life may depend upon it, you must have complete confidence that your equipment is in perfect condition.

Provided you act on the above advice, there is no need for you to buy a top-of-the-range buoyancy aid. These are often equipped with sophisticated pockets and chest-harness systems which are designed for experienced paddlers working in extreme white-water or expedition situations. They offer no special advantages to the beginner, so keep to simple, good quality equipment in the early stages.

If you are likely to be doing most of your paddling on coastal water, you should get a bright orange or red buoyancy aid. Being visible while at sea is an elementary safety precaution.

Clothing

The clothing requirements for canoeing depend a lot on the season, the weather, and the kind of paddling you are likely to be doing. One thing is certain: most water is cold, and you need to be protected if you are likely to be splashed or immersed in it! In an open canoe on a calm canal, you need hardly worry much about clothing, but if you are paddling in freezing white water, you must take it very seriously indeed. Here are the absolute basics you need to get started:

18

- A waterproof nylon anorak or cagoule. An ordinary walking or climbing jacket will serve until you have decided that canoeing is for you, but if you are staying with the sport, invest in one of the purpose-made "canoe cags" which have tight-fitting neoprene cuffs to stop the water running up your sleeves.

- Your swimming costume and a nylon track-suit bottom, preferably with a draw-cord waist.

- A tee-shirt and nylon track-suit top, plus a light woollen sweater for colder days.

- Well-fitting training shoes.

A purpose-made "canoe cag" is well worth buying during the early stages of your canoeing. Note the good seals at waist, neck and wrists, and the lack of pockets to fill up with water!

Wetsuits and drysuits

If you are intending to take up the kind of canoeing which involves getting wet often, a wetsuit will become essential to keep you warm. Wetsuits are made from foamed neoprene, a synthetic rubber which has thousands of tiny bubbles trapped within it and is an excellent insulator. When you get wet in one of these suits, a thin layer of water is trapped next to your skin: because it is sandwiched by the neoprene, the water is rapidly warmed by your body and remains at a comfortable temperature.

Neoprene wetsuits are buoyant, hard-wearing, and not at all uncomfortable to wear. A canoeing suit will normally be 3 mm ($\frac{1}{8}$ in) thick, with a sleeveless top and full-length trousers. When buying one, be sure that it has been made with canoeing in mind — the thicker material which scuba divers use will be too constricting. A good wetsuit will last for years.

Bootees made from neoprene wetsuit material are also readily available. These are very popular with white-water paddlers, who can expect to do a lot of walking around in rivers.

If you choose to paddle in a wetsuit, you stay quite warm if you just wear a swimming costume and light woollen sweater underneath, but always keep a nylon jacket or canoe cag handy for protection from wind.

Equipped for serious paddling, with a canoeing wetsuit worn over a sweater. The spray deck is pulled on like a skirt and fits snugly round the lower chest; when the paddler is seated, the elastic hem will be fitted to the lip of the cockpit, making a seal which will keep water out of the boat.

Paddlers venturing into extreme white water often use drysuits, which are all-enveloping oversuits with elastic seals at wrists and neck. The type you need for canoeing is a membrane drysuit; these are thin and allow unrestricted use of your arms. They are not in themselves very warm, so you wear a tracksuit or sweater and long-johns underneath, according to the air and water temperatures.

Drysuits will not stand as much rugged use as wetsuits, and have to be stored carefully. Don't rush into buying one before you are sure that it is what you need, and do make sure that the type you get is quite right for canoeing — models originally designed for sub-aqua use may not serve you well.

Spray deck

A spray deck is a waterproof fabric seal which fills the gap between the paddler's body and the edge of the cockpit. They are commonly made from proofed nylon.

Spray decks are used on kayaks to prevent water from entering the cockpit area in rough conditions. In winter, kayak paddlers on calm water also use them, as they help to trap warmth inside the boat.

The spray deck has two seals: one which fixes around the cockpit and a second which grips the paddler's trunk. The seals are usually elastic rope sewn into the nylon fabric. More expensive spray decks are made from neoprene and provide a much better seal. A cheap spray deck will be quite adequate for a beginner, but do remember that not all cockpits are the same size and you need to specify the type of kayak in order to get the right fit. Whatever sort you buy, it should have a release loop or tab to help when removing it from the cockpit rim.

Helmet

A helmet is not necessary for all canoeing activities, but if there is any chance of your head contacting the scenery or another boat, you must wear one. Helmets are made from a plastic shell, and usually have a foam liner inside. Although they are all adjustable, you may need to try several types in order to find one that fits you correctly and feels comfortable. It should be stable on your head, and the front rim should sit just above the bony ridge you can feel at your eyebrows.

A   B

Figure 7 Canoeing helmets: *A* is for normal use, *B* for extreme white-water conditions.

Helmets are essential in white-water canoeing or kayaking, surfing, canoe polo and slalom.

4

Basic techniques

Kayak and canoe paddling techniques are remarkably similar in feel. A proficient kayak paddler can transfer to canoe basics almost immediately. If you are a complete beginner in either a canoe or a kayak, spend a little time just sitting in your boat and experimenting with its movements and response to the paddle.

Kayaking techniques

Getting in and out

Figure 8 Getting into and out of a kayak or canoe

● Get the kayak floating alongside a straight piece of bank.

● Make sure that the paddle is on the bank within reach, and squat low until you can grip the centre of the front edge of the cockpit. Place your other hand on the bank.

● Keep your weight over the hand on the bank and put one foot into the kayak, on the centre line.

- Place your other foot in the boat, keeping low.
- Now drop your bottom onto the seat and tuck your knees in. Make sure that you take hold of the paddle before letting go of the bank!

Simply reverse this process when getting out.

Getting in and out: keep the boat against the bank, with your paddle close at hand. Note how the foot is placed on the centre line of the boat.

In kayaks with a very small cockpit, it is sometimes necessary to rest your weight on the rear deck while you slide your legs in.

When seated, make sure that your feet are firmly on the footrest. In a white-water kayak, additional location is also provided by having your knees in contact with the the underside of the deck.

Paddle grip

- Space your hands evenly to form a right angle at your elbows (see page 15).
- Right-handers — grip with your right hand so that the right blade pulls squarely through the water. To get the left blade in, swivel the shaft like a motor-cycle twist grip with your right hand and let it slip in your left hand.

● Left-handers — grip with the left hand and slip in the right.

The action needed to make the alternate blades enter the water correctly can feel clumsy and awkward at first, but within a very short time you will be able to handle it without even thinking.

Figure 9 Operating a kayak paddle: this one is controlled with the right hand.

Paddling forwards

● Sit upright and dip one blade at a comfortable reach.

● Pull the kayak past it and repeat on the other side.

● Let your trunk twist with each stroke.

● Let the top arm straighten while the lower arm pulls.

● Keep the action smooth and rhythmical.

Figure 10 Paddling forwards

Reversing

● Twist around and place a blade in the water behind you.

● Push the kayak past it and repeat on the other side.

● Look over your shoulder to see where you are going.

● Start with gentle strokes and move the kayak slowly.

Figure 11 Reversing

Emergency stops

If the kayak is running forwards and you need to stop quickly, use short, powerful reversing strokes. You should be able to stop dead in four strokes from any speed. Similarly, if you are reversing and need to stop, use positive forward strokes.

Turning

The *sweep stroke* is the most effective way of turning a kayak, and you will need to learn it early on. Practise at first with the boat at rest in still water before trying when it is moving.

Figure 12 The sweep stroke

● Grip the kayak firmly with your feet and knees throughout the stroke.

● Straighten your arm and reach towards your feet with the blade.

● Dig into the water so that the blade is fully immersed.

● Make a wide pull which moves the front of the boat *away* from the blade. Keep up the pressure until the blade is close to the rear of the boat.

● Lift the blade out and repeat the stroke on the same side, if necessary.

The reverse sweep is similar to the sweep stroke, but starts at the rear and moves forwards.

When you have got the feel of both strokes, try combining a forward sweep on one side with a reverse sweep on the other: this should make your kayak spin smoothly.

The stern rudder effect

This is a way of using your paddle as a rudder. It is a good way of steering the boat while it is running forwards, but it does not work unless the boat is moving at a reasonable speed.

● Get the boat running forwards, twist around and reach to the rear.

● Push the blade upright into the water parallel with the boat.

● Keep it close to the side of the boat, and let it trail.

● Push away from the side and watch the nose of the kayak come around.

● Rudder on the right to turn right, and vice versa.

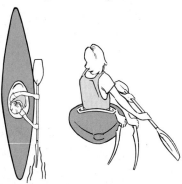

Figure 13 Using the paddle as a stern rudder

The stern rudder is used for fine steering only. More positive strokes such as the sweep are needed to make major turns. The stern rudder is a good stroke to learn when you are first trying to master the art of keeping a straight course.

Moving sideways — the draw stroke

Being able to move your kayak sideways is a very useful technique. The *draw stroke* demands a lot of practice to master, but the trouble is well worth it:

- With the kayak at a standstill, hold the paddle vertically with the blade parallel to the boat's side.

- Make sure the blade is totally immersed (this is called keeping a *deep blade*), pull hard, and sideslip the kayak towards it.

- Lift the blade out of the water as the boat draws up to it.

- Keep the boat running sideways by repeating the draw as often as necessary.

- Use a deep blade throughout.

- If you are making the draw correctly, your high arm will run across the top of your forehead.

Figure 14 The draw stroke

The support stroke

This stroke is used when you feel that you are going to overbalance. Once you have learned it properly you should never capsize accidentally!

Support strokes are an essential part of white-water technique.

- Sit upright and grip the kayak firmly with your feet and knees.
- Hold the paddle at chest height with one blade parallel to the water.
- Tip the kayak a little and let the blade slap onto the water surface.
- As the blade hits the water, drive the kayak upright with your knees.

The key to an effective support stroke is timing and confidence, so don't be afraid to practise.

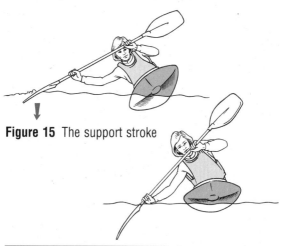

Figure 15 The support stroke

Practice tips

- Always try out new strokes on calm or very gently flowing water. A sheltered lake is perfect.
- Practise *all* the basic strokes, not just the ones which you find easy!
- Don't expect to learn these techniques in a few minutes; you need constant practice to learn properly.
- Set yourself targets, exercises and tasks which force you to use all the techniques — and take note of your improvement.
- As you improve, practise combining techniques so that you learn to link them smoothly and efficiently.
- Don't get disheartened if progress is slow; don't try to rush. If you just keep practising, you will learn — it's impossible not to!

Canoeing techniques

Launching

Canoes are usually more heavy and cumbersome than kayaks, so you may need help when moving them about on land. The usual method of launching is to let the water support one end while you slide the rest in gradually. This is a lot safer and easier if you have a line tied to the end that goes in last — especially when you are working from a high bank. Once the canoe is afloat, pull it alongside and get in using the method described for kayaks (see page 22).

Paddlers in canoes appear to be kneeling, but often the canoe has a seat on which you rest your bottom while your knees are also taking some of the weight. In open canoes the arrangement is wonderfully flexible, and various combinations of kneeling and sitting are possible.

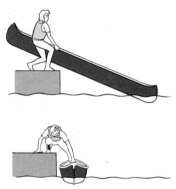

Figure 16 Launching an open canoe

Paddle grip

To find just where you should hold the paddle, try this method:

● Hold the T-grip with your dominant hand, and balance the paddle across your head. Your elbow should form a right angle.

● Grip the shaft with your other hand so that both elbows now form right angles.

● Lower the blade into the water.

This is your basic paddling position, but it may need a little adjustment later. It will allow you to paddle more easily on one side than the other, but don't feel you have to stick with this side — it is very useful to be good at the basic strokes on both sides.

Figure 17 The correct canoe paddle grip

Paddling forwards

This is a very relaxed and natural action. The main thing to remember is not to hold the paddle shaft too close to your chest. Guide the T-grip upwards at the start of the stroke and then let it descend as the stroke ends.

Figure 18 Paddling forwards

The J stroke

If you do nothing more than paddle forward on one side, the canoe will go around in a circle. The steering secret which allows a canoe paddler to hold a straight course without changing sides is called the J stroke. Here's how to do it:

● Start a normal forward stroke; as the blade passes your hip, rotate the T-grip through 45 degrees so that your thumb points forwards.

● Continue the movement backwards, but press outwards as well. This pulls the front of the canoe towards the side on which you are paddling.

● If you need to apply a more powerful turning force, press the shaft against the side of the canoe with your lower hand and lever the blade outwards as the boat glides along.

The sweep strokes

The sweep is a powerful turning stroke. You can make forward or reverse sweeps. For the forward sweep:

- Reach forward and press the blade into the water.

- Keep the shaft low, and pull in a wide arc; the canoe will turn away from the paddling side.

- Keep your arm straight throughout the pull.

- You can use the sweep to turn either a stationary or a running canoe.

Figure 19 The sweep stroke

The reverse sweep can be used when a turn towards the paddling side is required; the principles are the same, but you reach back to start the stroke.

Stern ruddering
When the canoe is running, you can control it by stern ruddering with the paddle, just as when kayaking. The T-grip of a canoe paddle makes this particularly easy.

The draw stroke
The draw moves the canoe sideways. There is a lot of drag when you do this, so the draw needs considerable effort.

- Kneel up straight, and turn to face the direction in which you want to sideslip.

- Keeping the T-grip high, place the blade in the water and pull it towards your hip.

- Lift the blade out of the water before the canoe and paddle meet, and repeat the action as often as necessary.

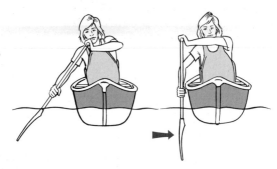

Figure 20 The draw stroke

The pry stroke

The pry is the opposite of the draw: it moves the canoe sideways, away from the side where you are paddling.

- Hold the blade upright in the water and with the shaft against the canoe side.

- By pulling the T-grip towards you, lever the canoe sideways. Then twist the blade so that it can slice back to its starting position, and repeat the cycle.

- Make the movement smooth and continuous, with the shaft remaining against the boat side throughout.

Support stroke

The support stroke is used to help you balance; it is particularly useful in rough water. In a canoe, the support stroke is very simple:

- Hold the paddle low, with the non-driving face of the blade (the side that would face forwards in the normal stroke) resting on the surface of the water.

- Just press down on the blade as necessary to steady the boat. You will be surprised how much support can be gained.

Figure 21 The support stroke

Doubles canoeing

Doubles canoeing is simple. The more expert paddler goes in the rear, from where the boat can easily be controlled by sweeping, J-stroking and stern ruddering.

Doubles canoeing is an excellent way of introducing disabled people to water sport. From the front of a two-seat canoe, visually or physically handicapped paddlers can enjoy the sport in safety.

Two-seater canoes are not the only way into canoeing for the disabled. Here, a young visually handicapped boy is being introduced to the sport by an expert BCU instructor.

5

The eskimo roll

Learning the eskimo roll is not essential for non-competitive paddlers, but if you can master it you will be able to take part in some of the more adventurous parts of the sport. It applies only to kayaks that are designed to roll — most other kayaks and canoes are very stable, and have larger cockpits so they cannot trap you if you do capsize: you just slip out as soon as you begin to lose balance.

When you first see a paddler rolling a kayak completely over and popping back to the surface sitting in the cockpit and still in control, the process seems almost magical — a complex and mysterious technique, far beyond the ability of normal human beings like you! This is not the case at all: anyone can learn to roll, provided that a progressive sequence of actions is followed. The trick is to break down the complete roll into its main stages, each of which can be practised and learned with ease, before attempting the whole technique.

Variations of the basic eskimo roll can be performed in most canoes and kayaks in which the paddler is located firmly in the cockpit, but here we describe only the single-seat kayak eskimo roll.

Preparation

You need to fit into the cockpit of your boat snugly. Your knees should be in contact with the braces under the deck, and your hips need to be touching the sides of the seat. Foam strips can be glued in place at these spots if there is too much space.

The ideal place to start is in a swimming pool. You will not need more than about 1.2 m (4 ft) of water, so there is no need to go out of your depth.

Wear swimming goggles or a diver's face mask; this will help you to remain orientated when the world turns topsy-turvy.

Always work with a partner standing in the water alongside, just in case you need an extra hand.

The six stages

Stage one: familiarisation
This is a simple matter of learning to hold your breath and remain calm when upside-down underwater. With your spraydeck in place, lean to one side and let the boat roll over while you try to remain in place for at least five seconds. Then you can either kick free and swim clear, or let your partner roll you upright again. Don't worry if you can't manage the full five seconds at first — keep trying until you can.

Stage two: the hip twist
The ideal place to try the hip twist is alongside the rail in a pool. If you can't do this, get your partner to hold a paddle shaft level with the surface of the water where you can grasp it.

Now grip the rail (or shaft) firmly and lean towards it until your shoulder is in the water.

Figure 22 The hip twist

Keeping your shoulder in the water, roll the boat as far onto its side as you possibly can, then bring it back to the upright position. Repeat this movement a few times and get used to the feel of the way your hips have to rotate to make the boat roll. This hip action is the key to the whole eskimo-roll technique: watch experienced paddlers, and you will see them use it every time.

Stage three: starting to use your paddle
Hold your paddle out to one side so that the blade is flat on the surface of the water. Get your partner to support the blade-end while you practise the hip action.

Start with very gentle oscillations, and gradually increase the range until you can capsize completely and then recover to a fully upright position.

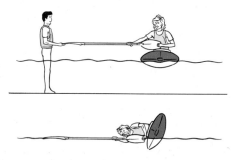

Figure 23 Using the paddle to help while practising the hip action

The rolling action should not require an enormous effort. A light, well-timed flick is all that is needed. If you find it is becoming a strenuous struggle, concentrate on the hip action — you may need to practise at the rail a few more times. Many learners find that leaning well back when applying the hip action makes things easier.

As your skill improves, your partner should gradually reduce support until you are managing without it.

Stage four: the set-up position

The position you take with your paddle at the very start of the roll is called the *set-up*. You have to become thoroughly familiar with the set-up, because it will act as a cue for the whole sequence of actions which your mind associates with the roll. Remember, you will not always be starting your rolls in calm, controlled conditions: you can easily become disorientated and confused when you go over in rough water.

To get into the set-up, lean well forward and hold the paddle shaft in line with the side of the boat. At first, grip the paddle towards one end, as illustrated for stage three. Get the blade which you prefer to use (usually the right blade for a right-hander) parallel to the surface of the water. When you are learning, you can take up the position when you are the right way up, on the surface, and hold it while capsizing. When you are completely capsized and stable, check your position again, then reach further around the side of the boat until your paddle breaks clear of the surface. The same blade should still be parallel with the water, and you should have retained the same grip. This is the set-up from which you can easily roll upright again.

When you set-up, make sure that the whole paddle shaft and the blade you are going to push with come completely clear of the water. Your partner can be a big help in checking that you have set-up correctly. If you use a face-mask or goggles, you will be able to see the surface and will understand just what direction you have to move the paddle in to get it into the air.

Stage five: the sweep

From the set-up, *sweep* the forward blade over the surface of the water until it is at right angles to the side of the boat.

Stage six: rolling up

Strike powerfully with the hip action while keeping a firm grip on the paddle; lean well back, and you will pop upright again. The whole action will be rather ragged at first, but with a little practice you will soon be able to bring your kayak upright and resume paddling without delay.

As you become better at rolling up, grip the shaft of the paddle nearer to the middle until eventually the whole exercise is performed without altering your normal paddling grip.

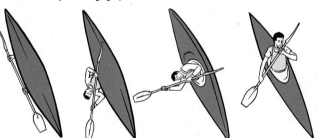

Figure 24 Rolling up

Rolling with full equipment

The next step is to practise the roll while wearing all your usual paddling clothing and equipment. You will find that this makes it rather more difficult to make a good set-up, and the all-important hip action is harder to achieve, but you must persevere.

Away from the bath

If all your roll training has been in a heated swimming pool, the final step is to try the exercise in a cold lake or river. This needs quite a lot of self-control: you must ignore the initial surge of cold water, and keep your mind on correct technique. Don't imagine that you have mastered the art of the eskimo roll until you can perform it reliably in cold conditions!

6

Competitive canoeing

Canoeing can be thought of as a number of almost separate sports, each with its own atmosphere, specialised equipment and structure. Some of these are energetic and exciting, while others are more peaceful and gentle. Many canoeists enjoy involvement in more than one aspect of the sport, finding that different kinds of satisfaction can be drawn from each. Most of the events operate a divisional system which allows canoeists of all standards to compete at their own level, with an incentive to move up to the next division. This works well, and ensures that beginners do not become disheartened by having to compete against experts.

In competition, the different classes of kayak and canoe are indicated by a simple code: *K* for kayaks, *C* for canoes, followed by a figure indicating the number of seats. Thus K2 is a two-seat kayak, C1 a single-seat canoe.

There are limits on the dimensions of the boats allowed in the different types of competition. This ensures that everyone is competing on the same basis, and prevents the development of unsafe freak boats.

Sprint racing

Sprint racing takes place on still water, usually on courses like those laid out for rowing regattas. Paddlers race against each other in lanes over distances ranging from 500 metres to 10 kilometres.

Sprint canoes and kayaks are designed purely with straight-line speed in mind. They are extremely light, and the cockpit space is large enough to allow the paddlers' legs freedom of movement with every forward driving stroke. Sprint kayaks are steered by the feet operating a rudder which hangs under the rear of the boat.

Pushing a racing boat along at top speed is exhilarating and physically very demanding. Good paddling technique involving rotation of the trunk is essential in both canoes and kayaks, and racing paddlers must train to develop the required upper-body fitness.

Flat-water kayak sprinters race their slim and relatively fragile craft in lanes.

Sprint racing is an Olympic sport, and the racing distances are:

Men: 500 m; 1000 m; 10,000 m
Ladies: 500 m; 6,000 m

Marathon racing

Marathon racing in canoes and kayaks is really very similar to road running, in that many people who take part are actually fun paddlers as opposed to serious racers. Naturally, the top end of long-distance paddling is very competitive and has its own world championships. However, most countries have a divisional system which allows people to compete with others of similar standards of fitness and speed.

Races take place on lakes, rivers and canals. Course distances vary from 16 km to 200 km (10–125 mi); the average is about 32 km (20 mi).

Above: A solo kayak marathon racer. This branch of canoeing has been described as "running with your arms".

Left: Solo and dual marathon kayaks at the end of a race.

In most events, paddlers in the lower divisions compete over a shortened version of the course. There are normally classes for kayaks and canoes, both single and doubles, and classes for males and females. Most races take place on gentle water, but some notable events, such as the notorious International Liffey Descent in Ireland, have rough sections containing rapids and weirs. One of the longest marathons is the world-famous Devizes to Westminster race, which crosses southern England by canal and finishes at Westminster Bridge on the Thames. The distance is 200 km (125 mi) and a fast time would be around sixteen hours!

The permitted dimensions of the boats used in marathons are the same as those for sprints; it is usual for paddlers to be involved in both types of racing.

Slalom

Slalom racing is a test of boat-handling skill on rough water. A course consists of around twenty-five "gates" suspended over a stretch of rapid river, and paddlers race individually against the clock to complete the course by passing through all the gates in the required order.

The gates consist of pairs of numbered and colour-coded poles. Red-and-white poles mean that the gate must be negotiated in an upstream direction, while green-and-white poles indicate a gate that should be passed through while paddling downstream.

In addition to a competitor's time from start to finish, time penalties are added for failing to pass cleanly through the gates. A penalty of five seconds is added for every gate touched; missing one completely, or going through in the wrong direction, results in a fifty-second penalty.

Because you have to break out of the main current repeatedly in the course of an event, and paddle against the stream at times, successful slalom racing demands lots of skill in controlling a boat in rough water, as well as a great deal of fitness.

You can start slalom paddling at any age, and many youngsters enter the sport through this branch.

As in most other types of competitive canoeing, races are held at various levels, according to the divisional system.

Slalom boats are light, and are designed with little depth between the deck and the bottom of the hull. This minimises the risk of hitting gate poles and gives the craft a lively and responsive feel in moving water. Firmly-attached internal buoyancy in the hull is essential, and the cockpit area must be shaped correctly to prevent the paddler becoming trapped by the legs.

Slalom racing is a test of speed and manoeuvrability on white water.

A slalom C2. This calls for teamwork of a high order.

All slalom racers must wear a crash helmet and buoyancy aid. It is very desirable but not absolutely essential to be able to perform the eskimo roll (see page 34).

Slalom-racing kayaks are good boats for introducing youngsters to kayaking skills. Being light and responsive, they make it easy to acquire the feel of paddling techniques. However, watch out for the sharply pointed ends of these boats, which can be a hazard to other paddlers.

Canoe polo

Despite the name, canoe polo is played in kayaks only. The rules are modelled on those of water polo, and most matches are held in swimming pools. There are two teams, each of five players, and scoring is achieved by getting the ball into the opposing goal.

Canoe polo is a fiercely competitive game with a strong international following. It combines tactical and ball-handling skills with the need for precise and agile paddling techniques. The ability to eskimo roll is important, as you frequently capsize as a result of legitimate tackling.

Polo kayaks are short (2–3 m; 6.5–10 ft) and have a width of approximately 55 cm (22 in). There are strict rules applying to equipment, play and safety. Paddlers must wear helmets and buoyancy aids, and many choose to wear face protection against accidental contact with opponents' paddles.

Canoe-polo craft are blunt-nosed for safety during close-quarter action. The sport demands fast boat handling and skilful ball control.

Wild-water racing

Wild-water racing is a fast and exciting sport in the same spirit as downhill ski racing — indeed, it used to be called down-river racing. The aim is to pick a line through the natural obstacles in a fast-flowing river which will take best advantage of the current; the skill is in holding that line while pushing the boat on at maximum speed. In a typical wild-water event, a course is determined over a length of white-water river and the

42

competitors set off individually on a time-trial basis. Organisers try to pick a course which will give a race time of about thirty minutes. The racers are given the chance to do a trial run down the course before the timed runs start.

The wild-water racing boat is designed with the emphasis on speed in a straight line, and it takes some time to develop the skill of steering in rough water. Naturally, competitors are required to wear helmets and buoyancy aids, and the boats need the same safety features as slalom racers.

In Britain, races are held in all regions where there are fast-flowing rivers. In other countries, the toughest wild-water events take place on alpine torrents. Sometimes the power authorities help by releasing water from hydro-electric dams to provide enough flow for good racing.

The classes are the same as those of slalom racing, and competitors are graded into divisions.

Wild-water racing: the boats are more buoyant than slalom craft, and so do not sit as low in the water.

C2 wild-water action

7

Non-competitive canoeing

Many people who love canoeing and kayaking have no desire to become involved in competition. They prefer the personal rewards of the experience itself, free from the restraints of competition.

Inland touring

Many countries have extensive inland waterways in the form of rivers, lakes and canals. Britain has several thousand miles of waterways, much of which is the old, but still magnificent, canal system. Mainland Europe is also served by extensive canal and river networks. A canoe or kayak is ideal for making long or short journeys on these waterways. Cities and open country are seen in quite a different light from the water, and most wildlife seems to be undisturbed by the quiet glide of a canoe — don't forget to take a camera! Virtually any type of craft will do for this kind of touring. Slim, lightweight racing craft cover the miles quickly and are easy to carry around locks and weirs, but wider and slower boats are more comfortable if you aren't concerned about getting anywhere quickly. You can carry basic camping equipment in all but the smallest craft.

An inland touring party on the River Spey in Scotland.

Open canoes or kayaks are perfect for journeys of any length on inland waterways.

White-water paddling

Paddling along rivers which contain stretches of white water is popular with kayakers. It is very much like mountaineering. You set yourself an objective such as completing a difficult section of river, or doing a long run on easy water just to enjoy getting out into wild country. White water is powerful and can be frightening, but getting into it and feeling the kayak take on the energy of the river is a habit-forming experience...

Running white water is tough on the equipment, and when the craft were made from wood or fibreglass they did not last long. The introduction of polyethylene hulls has caused a revolution in white-water canoeing. Now a good plastic boat will last for years and can easily tolerate the severe abrasion and compression which a beginner inevitably inflicts upon it while learning white-water skills. Polyethylene boats also suffer less from damage caused by travelling on trailers or roofracks — often a significant factor in the degeneration of a kayak.

The usual choice for white-water sport is a kayak up to four metres (13 ft) long, with a hull design which lets it turn fast and easily. The paddles need to be strong and hard-wearing to withstand the battering they will get in rocky rivers. A helmet, buoyancy aid and good spray deck are essential. As most white-water paddling takes place in winter or early spring, when there is plenty of water in the rivers, a good wetsuit is extremely important.

If you are going to venture onto white water, you should have learned how to perform an eskimo roll. This will give a tremendous boost to your confidence, and is also very important for safety, as it should prevent you from having to swim in difficult rapids.

Many of Britain's rivers offer superb white-water paddling. There are guide books for most regions which give full information on the accessibility and difficulty of the water.

White-water touring in the mountain rivers of Europe and North America is one of the most satisfying branches of canoe sport.

Sea touring

Sea touring in a kayak has been described as "a special kind of freedom". It is true: feeling the boundless size of the ocean from the cockpit of a tiny kayak sitting on its surface is a very special experience. You become aware of the proportions and forces of the natural world, and the problems of daily life shrink and disappear. In a sea kayak you can wander: trekking along the cliffs and beaches of the coast, or visiting islands that few other boats can get to. Your kayak can carry the comforts of food, clothing and camping equipment, and extended journeys of several weeks become possible.

While the sea is a beautiful place, it can also be extremely hostile. It is essential for the sea paddler to understand the sea, its movements and its relationship with the weather. You learn this by gaining experience in the presence of sea-kayaking experts. There is much to be discovered about planning, chart work, rescues and tides, but much of the fun is in the learning. Fortunately sea paddlers are warm and friendly people, and they are always willing to help enthusiastic beginners to learn to enjoy the sea safely.

Modern single-seat sea kayaks are between 480 cm and 510 cm (190–200 in) in length. Most have a small cockpit, and hatches in the deck leading to storage space in watertight compartments. Grablines are fitted to the deck. These become very important if you ever have to be rescued by another canoeist (see page 51).

If you take a few basic precautions, it is perfectly possible to use kayaks designed for other purposes on the sea. Those used for white-water paddling can deal with most conditions; their main limitation is lack of speed, but for short coastal trips they are fine.

Any kayak used at sea must have some form of grab handle at each end. This is an important safety precaution, as is the carrying of distress flares.

Sea touring around Scotland's Western Isles. Here the small canoes contrast with the towering black cliffs of Staffa.

A sea-touring party off the Isle of Anglesey, North Wales.

Surfing

Kayak surfing is a wild and exciting sport. The feeling of taking off from high on the face of a large green wave and catapulting down the wall of water has to be experienced to be believed. A kayak on a wave approaching the shallow water of a beach can be stood on end and shot into the air. It looks and feels mind-blowing, but it is in fact perfectly safe when you know what you are doing.

The skills demanded are very similar to those of white-water paddling, and the ability to roll is essential. White-water kayaks of the non-competitive kind work very well in surf, where their strength and resilience are put to the test.

When preparing a kayak for use in surf, all the un-occupied space in front and behind the paddler should be filled with flotation material (air bags or sealed foam). Make sure that the footrests are really strong too — the kind that supports the whole foot is recom-mended. A helmet and buoyancy aid are vital equip-mont and a strong paddle is essential.

Avoid beaches where the surf breaks over rocks, and don't be afraid to talk to local board surfers about any currents or underwater dangers which might not be obvious. Learn the skills from experienced paddlers, and never go canoe surfing alone.

Kayak surfing is an exhilarating sport for those who have already acquired good boat-handling skills. High speed and controlled aquabatics are possible in good surf.

8

Canoeing safety

As with any other outdoor sport, safe canoeing needs know-how, respect for the elements and a lot of common sense. No matter how skilled you may have become at handling your craft, if you are going onto unfamiliar water, always seek the advice of experienced local canoeists and take notice of it.

At first, you will be relying on other canoeists to help if you get into difficulties. However, as part of your involvement with the sport, you should learn basic canoeing first-aid and rescue techniques. You should also make a point of finding out about dangerous weather and water conditions, so that you do not always have to rely on the judgement of others where your own safety is concerned.

Ability to swim

Everybody who takes part in water sports should be able to swim, and canoeists are no exception. However, if non-swimmers are desperately keen to learn to canoe, and well-fitting buoyancy aids are available, they should be allowed to try the sport — it could provide the very incentive they need to learn to swim. A companion book in this series, *Take up Swimming*, is packed with straightforward help for non-swimmers of all ages.

Safety techniques

Capsize drill
Water confidence is something which goes beyond the simple ability to swim. This is particularly important for paddlers using canoes or kayaks with cockpits that enclose the knees, such as slalom, white-water or sea-going craft. In these boats you need to learn how to deal with being upside-down while underwater, as when capsized. Panic in such circumstances is dangerous — what is needed is calm, well-practised action.

You can build up your water confidence in the controlled conditions of a swimming pool, which is also the best place to learn capsize routines (see page 34). Learning to eskimo roll is a natural extension of water-confidence practice.

Deep-water rescue

If you capsize in deep water you can get back into your canoe or kayak if you are with a partner who knows the deep-water rescue technique. Such a rescue is only possible, however, if you have kept hold of your boat and paddle, a habit you must drill into yourself.

The key to deep-water rescue is practice. It helps if both the rescuer and the canoeist in the water know the stages:

● The swimmer holds onto the rescuer's boat and helps the rescuer to get hold of one end of the capsized boat.

● The rescuer then pulls the capsized craft over the cockpit area of his own boat, to drain the water from it. (Not into his boat, of course!)

● The rescuer turns the now-empty boat upright and slides it back into the water. The two boats should now be side-by-side.

● The swimmer gets between the two boats, facing in the direction his boat is pointing. He swings his feet into his cockpit while pulling the two kayaks together under his back. The rescuer steadies the boats as far as possible until the swimmer is seated again.

Although the most common use for this rescue is between kayaks, the system works with open canoes too.

Figure 25 Throughout a deep-water rescue, the swimmer must never lose contact with the boats.

Water hazards

Stoppers

A stopper is a vertical eddy that develops underwater downstream of a weir or submerged rock. The water can be rolling back onto itself in such a way that canoes or swimmers can be trapped and held under at this point. Large stoppers can be extremely dangerous.

Weirs

Weirs are man-made walls built into the bed of a river to regulate the flow. The water can appear placid just above a weir, but as it flows over the wall, stoppers are set up below the weir. These can capsize a canoe or kayak and trap the paddler. Even wearing a buoyancy aid, a swimmer in this kind of water is in grave danger of drowning, and anyone who tries to offer assistance may well suffer the same fate.

Weirs are common on many rivers, and you should assume that they are all dangerous to canoeists. The only safe action is to stay well clear of them.

Canoeists should keep clear of weirs of any size.

Pollution

It is a sad reflection of our times that many rivers in developed countries carry harmful pollutants. In all but the most sedate forms of canoeing you will probably come into contact with the water, so try to shower or at least wash thoroughly after paddling. Any cuts or broken skin should be covered while on the water, and rinsed afterwards.

If you develop flu-like symptoms after a session on the river, contact a doctor and tell him when and where you were canoeing.

Graded water

Rivers containing white water are graded according to difficulty, from I to VI:

● Grade I: Slow-moving water with shallows

● Grade II: Irregular flow, with small waves and eddies

● Grade III: Irregular waves and stoppers; the route to be followed is easily recognisable.

● Grade IV: Continuous heavy rapids; large boulders may obstruct the stream. The route is not clear.

● Grade V: Very difficult water with large waves, stoppers and drops

● Grade VI: Extreme white water posing a serious threat to life

Dealing with emergencies

Although canoeing is basically a safe sport, you must be able to help someone who appears to have stopped breathing, either through drowning or impact. The first-aid techniques you need are *artificial respiration*, which restores breathing, and *external chest compression* to restore the pulse. Both these techniques are easy to learn, but are beyond the scope of this book: good canoe clubs organise first-aid evenings at which you can practise them on a lifelike dummy.

If an accident occurs, get the victim on land and get medical help quickly.

Hypothermia

Hypothermia is often referred to as *exposure*; it is a condition caused by losing too much heat from your body. You can reach this state by becoming exhausted in cold weather, or by immersion in cold water, or both.

Sufferers from the early stages of hypothermia look pale, may be shivering, and often stumble when they try to walk. If they are kept dry and wrapped up warmly inside a shelter, they will usually recover quite quickly. If they continue to cool, however, they are likely to become seriously ill.

The secret is to prevent hypothermia from happening by taking simple precautions:

● Wear warm, windproof clothing when canoeing.

● If you are likely to capsize or otherwise get very wet, wear a wetsuit and canoe cag.

● Don't attempt a canoeing venture which might be too much for you.

53

- Food is fuel; it plays an important part in maintaining your body temperature, so don't miss meals.
- Stop and get ashore before you get exhausted.

If you suspect that a member of your party is at risk from hypothermia and is not re-warming through natural exercise, *you* must help:

- Make the subject stop and put on more clothes.
- If there is no obvious shelter nearby, provide some by getting the victim into a survival bag and huddling tightly around him or her, using the boats as a windbreak if necessary.
- Keep talking to and encouraging the victim.

Canoeing first-aid

First-aid kit
Always carry a simple first-aid kit with you in your canoe, and keep it dry and clean in a small plastic container. The kit should include:

- A small roll of surgical tape
- Some fabric sticking-plasters
- One or two wound dressings, sealed in polythene
- A crepe bandage
- A small pair of scissors

Full equipment for a non-competitive white-water paddler: the basic emergency kit consists of a first-aid kit, knife, spare sweater, repair tape, throwline and survival bag, all kept in a waterproof bag. On extended or wilderness journeys, spare paddles are carried too.

Blisters, cuts and grazes

The most common first-aid problem in canoeing is blisters on the hands. Beginners almost always get them at first, but the skin very soon adapts by forming a hard pad where the blisters occur. If you feel blisters coming on, cover the area with a clean pad held by canoe tape or a sticking-plaster. Cover cuts and grazes with a wound dressing, applying direct pressure.

Weather forecasts

When you are preparing for a day's canoeing, knowing the weather forecast is just as as important as getting the equipment ready. Extremes of weather can have a serious effect on your day. You should know what weather to expect, and act accordingly. You *must* be prepared to change your plans or even abandon the trip completely if necessary. This advice is particularly vital if you are planning to go sea canoeing; sea conditions are almost totally dependent on the weather. Useful sources of weather forecasts in Britain are:

- Television — usually after the news.

- Radio: BBC Radio 4 gives the shipping forecasts four times daily, as well as regular detailed general forecasts. They also broadcast an excellent forecast for coastal water conditions very late at night (about 12.30am).

- British Telecom Weathercall and Marinecall services (24 hours.)

- HM Coastguard service: look up the number in the phone book.

- The daily newspaper. It is surprising how many sportspeople overlook the fact that some papers print a very good weather chart.

Coastguards

The coastguard service will help canoeists to safeguard themselves on sea journeys, but they cannot do anything if they do not know about you. You do not have to advise the coastguard before every trip, but do make sure that *someone* competent knows:

- Where you are going
- How many of you there are in the party
- When you will be off the water
- What distress-signalling equipment you are carrying

Tell them to contact the coastguard if you become over-due. The telephone number will be in the local directory; or, in emergency, dial the emergency number (*999* in the UK).

Lifting and transporting

Canoes and kayaks can be heavy and awkward loads to lift. Take care when you lift, and get assistance if necessary — don't tackle a load which may be too much. Avoid the risk of back injury by always taking the weight with your leg muscles, not your back muscles. An injured back could totally ruin your future as a paddler.

You can drain a kayak on your own, but the task is much easier if there are two of you.

The easiest way to lift and carry all but the largest canoes singlehanded is by first setting the boat up onto its edge and then holding it by the edge of the cockpit, rather like a suitcase. Most single-seaters balance at this point, and you can often rest them on your shoulder, with your arm inside. Quite long distances can be covered carrying the canoe this way.

Roofrack sense

Get help when lifting a heavy boat on or off a roofrack.

Take great care when tying your boat onto the rack. A boat leaving a roof at speed is a lethal missile and could cause a multiple road accident. It won't do a lot for the boat either! Check that the rack is securely attached to the car, and use bolt-on uprights or V-bars to prevent lateral movement. Use only strong nylon rope or purpose-made self-locking tapes to secure the boats. If you are using ropes, learn how to tie reliable knots — don't chance to luck by making something up on the spot. A clove hitch or a round turn and two half hitches will secure most loads.

Don't take chances with boats on a roof-rack. Use a good-quality rack, strong rope and sound knots. This rack has also been fitted with simple bolt-on uprights which increase security immensely.

Nylon straps with self-locking buckles are a good investment if you are going to carry canoes frequently.

9

Getting started

Fortunately for keen newcomers, canoeists love to get people interested in their sport. They enjoy teaching and are often willing to let beginners borrow their equipment — they understand that everyone has to be a beginner at some stage. This is good news for you, because what you need is to try out canoeing before going to the expense of buying your own boat.

Even if you are able to buy all the equipment and provide your own transport, the best way to start is still to attach yourself to a canoeing group of some sort. Paddling alone, even on placid water, is not safe until you know a lot more about the sport.

The perfect introduction to the sport: an open-cockpit "placid water" kayak.

Find a group

Canoeing is now so widespread that there are clubs almost everywhere within a reasonable distance of water. Often, schools have their own canoe clubs, and many Scout and Guide groups have access to a regional fleet of canoes or kayaks.

Joining a club and working with other paddlers is important for safety, as well as being a great way to progress in the sport. These young competitors are taking part in their first team slalom.

There are also general canoe clubs, outdoor centres running canoeing courses, and commercial organisations which offer short canoeing sessions. If you have any difficulty finding a club, enquire at your local public library, or contact the national governing body or (in Britain) your regional Sports Council office. Also, don't be shy: you will often see cars with canoes on the roofrack: if you have a chance to talk to the driver, you will probably have found an enthusiast. Don't be afraid to approach someone like this for guidance on local canoeing. People love to see enthusiasm, and paddlers enjoy helping each other out.

Apart from the help and guidance you will receive from a club, you will probably find that there is organised transport which you can share. Clubs often run expeditions to different areas so that you can widen your experience early on.

Another advantage of paddling with others is that you can learn from them. Formal teaching is not the only way to learn; you will improve very quickly just by watching your fellow paddlers and then having a go yourself. Set yourself goals, based on what you see more experienced paddlers doing, and work with determination towards reaching each goal.

Swimming-pool practice

Many swimming pools allow organised groups to run canoeing sessions. As a beginner, you will find that these are of great benefit, particularly if you are likely to be paddling a white-water or slalom kayak. The warm, clean water of the pool allows you to explore the boat and its balance, and to learn to capsize without fear. This is the best place to develop your grip on the cockpit, to practise support strokes of all kinds and to master the eskimo roll.

Practice in the pool offers you the opportunity to keep learning through the winter months when the weather might otherwise keep you off the water. Sometimes canoeing sessions are announced on the notice boards at your local pool or leisure centre.

Boats are usually supplied at these sessions, but if you have your own paddle and spray deck, make sure they are quite clean and take them along. A nose clip and swimming goggles are handy to have as well, and take a track-suit top into the pool area in case you need to sit around.

The swimming pool is also the perfect place for disabled people to start canoeing.

You don't have to live by a river to take up canoeing! The swimming pool is an excellent training ground for developing confidence and learning new skills.

Keep learning

You can learn a lot about the sport by reading books and watching videos and films. This will help you to decide what types of canoeing you would like to specialise in once you have mastered the most basic skills.

Remember, the very early stages of learning to paddle are the toughest. You may sometimes feel silly, and will probably soon get tired: but keep at it! This phase does not last long, and soon you will find yourself controlling your boat without even thinking about it.

Disabled canoeists

Guidance for disabled people coming into the sport is available in the UK from the British Canoe Union and the British Sports Association for the Disabled (BSAD). There are several types of canoe which have been developed specially for disabled paddlers, and other boats can be made suitable with minor modification. The BCU has published a booklet containing full information and guidance on the subject.

Finding out more

International Canoe Exhibition

In Britain, one of the best ways of finding out what is available on the canoeing market is to visit the International Canoe Exhibition which is held each February at the Crystal Palace Sports Centre in London. The event lasts for a full weekend, and every piece of equipment you can imagine is on display and available for sale. The weekend includes films and slide talks, competitions of all kinds in the swimming pool and a canoe-polo league final.

As well as seeing all the equipment, you can meet your BCU regional representative. All the different disciplines in the sport are represented by experts too, so you can get answers to all your questions under one roof.

British Canoe Union

The British Canoe Union is in charge of the sport in Britain. The BCU covers all the different canoe and kayak disciplines, and operates many coaching schemes via regional representatives. The Union also protects the interests of all canoeists, and is an active campaigner for the right of access to more water. If you contact the BCU office at the address on page 64, they will send you a list of clubs and contacts in your area. Initial enquiries will cost you nothing, and once you have become active in the sport you will probably want to become a member.

Many other countries have similar organisations, and a list of the main ones appears at the back of this book.

Canoeing Handbook

The *Canoeing Handbook*, published by the BCU, is the most comprehensive English-language manual of the sport. It contains information on all canoeing disciplines, as well as interesting reading about the history of canoeing and guidance on how to teach and lead groups.

10

Buying your first boat

New canoes and kayaks

Now that you have read as far as this, you will have realised that simply going into a shop and attempting to buy a canoe is not the best starting point. You must have an idea of where your area of interest in the sport lies, or you will almost certainly end up with the wrong boat. Of course, you may be absolutely certain that you intend to go into, say, slalom racing, in which case you need a pure slalom canoe or kayak; end of story! However, if you are not certain, look hard at the range of canoe sport which your locality offers and do your best to try everything, then buy a boat that allows for several possibilities. For example, a simple white-water kayak is often a good choice: in one of these you can tour canals, ride the surf, make coastal journeys and even compete in slalom races. Check that any boat you buy complies with the dimension regulations for your chosen class.

The market in secondhand boats is quite active, so if you do decide later to specialise, you should not have much trouble selling your original canoe or kayak.

Do take your time before parting with your money for a new boat. Read the canoeing magazines, and talk to lots of people about the different types and methods of construction.

There is no substitute for "trying before buying", and a good retailer will have demonstration boats. Also, look out for deals which are offered from time to time, such as a complete package which includes the boat, paddle, spray deck and buoyancy aid for a really good price. These are well worth considering, but do get equipment which fits you properly — don't accept anything else. In Britain, look for the label of the British Association of Canoe Traders on new boats as a guarantee of production-quality and service.

Secondhand equipment

Unlike used cars, which have lots of hidden parts that cannot easily be inspected, with secondhand canoes and kayaks you can nearly always see what you are getting. This makes secondhand buys quite safe, but you obviously need to have an idea of what to look for:

● Check the skin of the boat for obvious ruptures which will leak as soon as it is in the water. Fibre-glass boats may well have repair patches on the hull, and this is quite normal. If a patch is hanging off, or is soft and spongy, it will probably be a source of trouble in the form of both leaks and weakness. Each patch adds weight, so avoid boats which have too many patches.

● Holes in polyethylene boats are rare, but the material is much harder to repair than GRP. If you are considering buying a polyethylene boat with visible damage, do get expert advice before paying up.

● Some secondhand boats will have lost their internal flotation foam. You can buy replacement foam and restore such a boat yourself, but make sure that the price you pay allows for this. Get expert advice on fitting the foam, and never be tempted to use any boat without internal flotation.

● Don't forget to inspect the footrest, particularly when buying a kayak; be sure that it will adjust to suit your leg length.

Secondhand boats are advertised in canoeing magazines, on club noticeboards, at events such as competitions, and sometimes in retail shops.

Used white-water kayaks
If you are buying a kayak with the intention of using it on white water, you must be especially careful:

● The internal flotation foam must be of the high-density type — polyethylene, not polystyrene.

● The foam must be very secure — not loose.

● The footrest should be strong, and designed so that neither of your feet can become trapped behind it. This can happen with the single-bar type of footrest, which should be avoided.

● The cockpit area must be free from cords or rope which could entangle you as you exit. For the same reason, if decklines are fitted, they must not continue alongside the cockpit.

Useful addresses

British Isles

The British Canoe Union
Mapperley Hall
Lucknow Avenue
Nottingham NG3 5FA

Irish Canoe Union
4/5 Eustace Street
Dublin 2
Ireland

Canoe Association for Northern
    Ireland
House of Sport
Upper Malone Road
Belfast BT9 5LA

Scottish Canoe Association
Caledonia House
South Gyle
Edinburgh EH12 9DQ

Welsh Canoe Association
Pen y Bont
Corwen
Clwyd LL21 0EL

Overseas

American Canoe Association
8580 Cinderbed Road
Suite 1900
PO Box 1190
Newington, Virginia
USA

Australian Canoe Federation
Room 510
Sports House
157 Gloucester Street
Sydney, NSW 2000
Australia

Canadian Canoe Association
333 River Road
Vanier City, Ontario K1L 8B9
Canada

Fédération Française de Canoe
    Kayak
17 Route de Vienne
69007 Lyon, France

New Zealand Canoeing
    Association
PO Box 3768
Wellington, New Zealand

International

Fédération Internationale de Canoe
Sarajevska 22/1
YU-11000 Beograd
Yugoslavia